# The Crooked Truth

**Selected Poems by Dan Guenther**

2010

ISBN 1-933704-05-5

Printed in the United States of America
Cover design by Ingrid Guenther
Author photo by Dave Scott

## Acknowledgments

In Part I of this collection are poems written while I lived in Australia that were published in the journals, *Poetry Australia* and *Quadrant*. In Part II I've included two poems published in *Buffalo Bones*, a small magazine that was once published in Evergreen, Colorado, as well as four poems from the anthology *Turning Up The Leaves* (Coe Review Press, 2000). I hope these selected poems show an evolution over the years, reflecting both personal growth, and a sense of the times during which the poems were written.

In addition, I would like to recognize the support I've received since the Seventies from the poets Les Murray and Norman Dubie. Their interest has encouraged me to complete this book. Also, I would like to thank Dow Mossman, Ed Gorman, Carolyn Evans Campbell, Wayne Karlin, and Steve Kennedy for their input on this manuscript. As well, thanks to my daughter, Ingrid, her husband Dave Scott, and my wife, Cheryl, for their thoughts and perspectives over the years.

# Table of Contents

## Introduction

Dan Guenther is a poet for all seasons who speaks to us through unique imagery and often brilliant contrast about his many years walking the western landscape, the old Ute trails in Colorado, foreign lands, and a war-torn countryside. His deep relationship with the natural world, and all its creatures has a way of healing, making connections, and balancing one's life in the great scheme of living and dying. In silence and solitude and in secret places, from Vietnam to a winter campsite, he ponders the big questions, and we listen. His meditations on time, space and light, ancient cliff dwellers and new beginnings, awaken the poet in us. We feel his compassion and respect for all things living…and dead. The world of the night heron, wolverine, mule deer, and lynx, all hold mystical truths for him.

> *Lately animals and birds appear in my dreams, clothed as human beings along with the ghost of a drowned child.*
>
> *Maybe it is true that divinity lies dormant within us, a mystery waiting to rise again from the ages, from the marble pagodas of Vietnam to these eroded sandstone shapes once worshipped by Utes.*

We are grateful when he says *the child in me still believes in magic*, because on each page of this fine collection, we believe with him.

Carolyn Evans Campbell, author of *The Tattooed Woman*, Colorado Book Award winner

# Part I: Trail Dust

## Trail Dust

*For Cheryl*

I returned from Asia to work high up in the Yellowstone,
and fell in love with the remote backcountry,
the raw unexpectedness of it, the moments
that pulled me from my deep melancholy
at a time when no serene oriental words of wisdom
could free me.

At each sunrise I would look down the long valley of my past
to see what dark horsemen were gaining in their pursuit.

Many a night, staring into the campfire,
I pondered the random and unnamed zones I'd traveled,
some wet, dark and tropical,
others eroded, bright, and water-worn,
ready to ignite at the slightest spark.

Things in their cycle must fade in order to be born again;

And I stared into those fires until my heart cracked open,
the heat burning away those traces
of other times and places that dogged my temperament.

When that summer was over I learned to acknowledge
what I called my limitations,
and was ready to mingle with people once again:

The only thread in this narrative worth remembering
for a mind displaced by time and old age
is our own story;
and beyond that, you don't have to understand,
just continue on believing
that love is the only path beyond grief.

It will be you who will carry my trail dust home when I'm gone.

Sprinkle a bit on your pillow
in memory of how you took my breath away.

## After the Burn

The wildfire caught the winds just right
along the Front Range north of Denver,
riding side by side with those angry, up-slope spirits
that always arrive after the thaw.

When a dark plume loomed over our ridgeline
the magpies screamed retreat,
and the fire picked up speed, the junipers exploding,
our appaloosa spooked and running down Highway 93.

When help finally came to form a fire line
at the ancient cottonwoods it was almost too late,
and we were humbled and soaked with sweat,
grateful that at least the giant trees were spared.

The wildfire swept away our barn and the big bluestem
we took ten years to restore, lifted everything skyward
in a spiral of ashes, leaving a black scar
where both Utes and Arapahoes once grazed mustang stock.

We could rage across that blacken space,
but the realizations have come too late for pondering
what else could have been done to save all that
which has been lost.

In the morning a light rain fell, settling the dust,
and gazing up at the gnarled trunks,
we took comfort in knowing this grove should live on
long after we're gone.

A sacred place to the Utes, my father always talked
about the sweet spring flowing from among the cottonwoods,
and how the breeze in the shimmering leaves high overhead
reflected dapples of light on the surface of the water:

Sometimes we stand alone, waiting
on a separate, dream-struck plain,

trying to remember the best of times while our heart aches,
and our mind shifts, devoid of any acuity or understanding.

## Water Dreams

Broad wings of the wind bring rain,
and you float on the dark,
lying awake,
waiting for dawn
and the return of that sky-floater,
the red-tailed hawk.

Understand that no answers
ever arrive at this late hour.

But years from now, on a hot, dry afternoon,
you will recall how the night breeze
turned into a cool, swift current
with its promise of tomorrow,
and how you were caught and carried off
into water dreams,
while listening to the rain.

In the early hours out on that broad river
beyond the hills,
giant catfish sleep as they drift downstream.

**Zones**

At this elevation, where your cell phone barely connects,
a pika owns the boulder field,
and he scurries away across the krummholz.

He stores his crystalline urine in a sparkling cache,
and forages for fireweed while you check your voice mail.

Up in the alpine zone strange things affect phone reception.

The feeble background static you hear is the primordial hiss
of ancient microwaves, left over from the dawn of time.

Not far below, where a hundred elk shelter together,
a half-butchered carcass blocks the trail.

A man in a hooded sweatshirt lugs a hindquarter into the trees
no doubt one of the meat-hunters living off the land,
and cooking his meth somewhere in the backcountry.

You wonder how many other predators may be watching.

In this high terrain
each step is taken with uncertainty,
and in the trembling quiet of our dim, ancestral memories.

The chirping pika sounds a alarm,
scolding all the intruders in his anonymous domain,
from deep within the shade of an altitude-stunted spruce.

## Elegy for the Cicadas

After such a long sleep
the cicadas climb into the treetops
where dark oaks rise like religious towers.

The heat of the day softens their stiff tongues,
and they lift their wings to sing,
turning loose the longings of seventeen years.

We belong to their brief cycle,
to that whine for the chirping nymphs
emerging from the leaf-litter,
when all that runs and cries is bright and young.

So what form is this that broods to shed its skin,
then clicks in our memory, perennial as a first kiss,
to tangle together high on the trunks of trees,
buzzing until they perish and we are sleepless?

The wind gathers their crisp remains,
sweeping all that falls to earth into ashen clusters,
food for the grumbling toads scavenging within the ferns.

## Finding Refuge

In dense woods
where the weasel's red eye gleams,
blue jays pick clean the carcass of a deer.

Light rain slicks the trillium and bloodroot.

Last night, in their estuary of leaves,
tree frogs croaked.  A circle of pale toadstools
sprung up
under the canopy of the oaks.

The blue jays protest our passage forward.

Tangles and leaf litter hide the refuge of the vole.

Just ahead, where the weasel speeds on,
aligned only with his dark design,
the clear-eyed and chattering jays
protest the dark snout nosing in the leaves,
the chilly wind's needle teeth.

**Elegy for the Frog Choir**


Twilight dissolved into an April moon,
and you took her pony for a ride
to a pond bordering the deep woods.

You were gangly and dumb, both tall for your age,
playing with fire
while chorus frogs trilled along the reedy banks.

When the wind in the trees picked up speed
so did she, guiding your hand in that dark hour
to the songs of a frog choir.

The pond dried slowly into mountain meadow
over time, and the ranks of the frog choir
have thinned to disease and ultra-violet rays.

High overhead, on silent wings,
flocks of geese glide by, the old pond
but an ancestral memory in their cold celestial blur.

Out in the snowy timber
the call of a great horned owl
fades in the moonlit here and now.

**After the Thaw**

A pale opossum travels along our river through the night,
and he stares back at me in the moonlight,
caught once again in our garbage,
his soulful face like that of a lost spirit.

For a second year in a row he has returned
after the thaw, ushering in spring's divine rains.

This drab beggar carries off our waste as an offering
to his unnamed deities, and for all we know
he could be counting the risings of Venus
on the delicate toes of his tiny paws.

Lately animals and birds appear in my dreams, clothed
as human beings, along with the ghost of a drowned child.

And recently I was told
the wild bees have all but disappeared from our valley.

That nest robber, the loggerhead shrike,
sighs from among the thickets of scarlet haw lining
the river's banks; and he shakes in his restless sleep,
his head spinning with dark schemes.

During the hot afternoons he retires to his shady keep,
impaling the still trembling young
of other birds upon those wicked thorns
hidden in the density of the leaves.

Why is it we always feel that inevitable ache
for the lost in the darkness of the night?

Our river flows on, bearing its quiet burdens, and at daybreak
the swallows will be skimming across the surface of the water.

**At First Light**

For thirty years I've followed old trails
used by the Mountain Utes,
tracking wildlife through the snow,
often at first light.

Every year I walk the high meadows
to where the bull elk shed their antlers,
the magpies scolding me through the scrub-oaks.

While the weather is still cool,
and before the snakes come out,
I find new paths along the Front Range
where the deer bed down to watch the lights
stretching away across the plains.

My wounds have taken a lifetime to heal, my symptoms
following a cycle with the seasons, perspectives
changing, then shifting back:

When the high country is swept by sudden rain,
with Denver's office towers glinting in the distance,
Southeast Asia seems no more than an abstraction,
a history as cryptic as the rock pictures
left by the ancients along the Arkansas.

Up here, for a time, a mind can leave behind
what remains unresolved, to find the kingfisher
tunneling into a narrow bank within a dark canyon,
and glimpse the otters on their muddy slick.

Some habits are hard to break, and a natural inclination
takes me down old trails: but I no longer believe
that everything is lost with death.

## Chronicles from the Whale's Road

I once ran away looking for oil
to make Norway proud again, and off the Orkneys
rode the rainy swells of the Whale's Road.

We drank Russian vodka,
longing for old times
while the world credit crisis propelled us toward collapse,
and while Olaf, our captain,
lulled us to sleep with his chronicles
of the ancient Norse singing in their great halls:

All I know is captured in a single computer image,
the fruits of my sonic scanning, blinking
and luminescent green,
an opaque troll's eye
peering into the depths,
guiding us to geologic domes hidden in this codless sea.

One clear night I climbed with several of our crew
up onto the ship's rigging
to watch the Northern Lights.

Our Chinese engineer then told me
in his cosmology there was no creator,
and no higher plane of meaning beyond the here and now.

A pod of those rare, beaked whales passed by below us,
gliding on the shimmering water toward Iceland
where herring and squid still swarm, from a distance
their breaching spume, pure and uncorrupted, icy plumes
suspended high above the waves like so many
shape-shifting spirits, or a sign from Odin.

## Humpback Whales

*From Quadrant, 2008*

Whalers called their songs
the dark liturgy of Lucifer,
the grunts and groans of his aggrieved,
fallen angels, echoing
through the scalloped chambers of the ships.

Off Hawaii, long ago, I first heard them cry
from their cathedral in the deep.

The songs bring their solitary kind together.

And together the sonic pods
become acrobats, cavorting,
leaping free and clear-eyed,
high into the air,
shaking barnacles from mottled snouts.

At times the placid humpbacks will float quietly
on the smooth surface of a night sea.

Do you suppose the whales are gazing at the stars,
the galaxies spinning
above them in cosmic emptiness?

## Elegy for Jock

In a previous life I crossed the border
from Thailand into Cambodia,
back to those smoky barrooms
where the social misfits and morally bankrupt
mixed in deadly crowds to sell their skills.

Even now as glaciers in the Himalayas melt down,
and the Mekong flows
quiet and lazy, merging with rivers
whose names I have forgotten, primeval ruins loom
out of the broad, flat plains of my memories:

When Jock committed suicide in Phnom Penh,
his Khmer wife danced for days before
a floor-length mirror, wild-eyed, her black hair flying
like that of a sorceress, her blade-thin body sweaty
and glistening in a haze of incense and candlelight.

"He has already returned in the incarnation
of a cat, of that I am confident," she snapped at me.

"You will find him at that cosmic intersection
he often spoke about, mingling with celestial nymphs
from other galaxies who change their shape at will,"
she said, twirling, her madness quite complete.

So we wept one last time for Jock, our Australian mate,
two Yanks having found and recovered his remains.

Jock, who all his life yearned to understand infinity,
who believed in a Karmic chain
woven intimately into everything,
who believed that beauty
offered the only path through the darkness.

## Letter from the Plains of Central Asia

Many come here for the healing waters,
others to escape the void.

Some to connect with lost mysteries under the palms.

At its height this city boasted ten thousand under arms,
fountains of artesian water for the spice caravans,
always a city looming large in my historian's eye.

Nights on the broad avenues belonged to street musicians
and poets, philosophers who argued various possibilities
of being, the unchanging within the flow of sensibility.

But the king's astronomers turned to prophesy
and a false science of the stars,
evoking decadent forms in their path to power,
beauty, decay, and rebirth, the transcendent ethic.

The end came out of the cold steppes to the north.

A vigorous horse culture, yet to be degraded,
swept down on hardy ponies to seize the wells.

Tall horsemen took control, marveling at the comfort
found in this city on the plains,
and embracing that dark Gnosticism
with its worship of black angels.

Dusty tombs chronicle the history of their slow decline,
where I consumed my life in a worthless study.

My life has contributed nothing to the greater good.

When you read this letter I will have walked away
into the treeless nothingness beyond the walls.

How appropriate for the shape-shifter I have become,

dying in the pursuit of a more complete knowledge,
and perhaps crossing into another world…

## Cabbage Palmettos

I lost my way
wandering inland off the beach,
curious about a pipeline oozing toxic waste
among the exotic cypress and lurking cottonmouths.

In the shallows great blue herons eyed echelons
of silver sickle-backs
as the environmental links broke down;

And my neurotransmitters needed more medication.

Watching the deft swallows circle in the afternoon,
over the cabbage palmettos lifting in the breeze,
has a way of regulating my moods.

But I know that I am going daft.

A residue is hovering just off shore in a cloud,
suspended within the currents
like a fragile fairy shrimp, about to be carried away.

## Elegy for an Uncle Lost in the Oil Rich States

All your life you traded with the oil rich states,
and in 1938 were among the first
to tap the reservoirs out in that hopeless void.

While the black swill poured forth like a flood
you shaped modern history,
and sanitized the truth:

We are all placed at a slightly different angle
to the light, and thus none of us sees things the same way
when the wealth of nations is pumped from the ground.

Call the Devil in your Faustian bargain the petrodollars
offered by your subtle princes, the same ones who squandered
fortunes on blond fantasies and custom Mercedes.

Oh, you were very good in your wary craft, creating schemes
and arranging scenarios,
with nothing but time on your hands.

Oil was your intoxicant, a black gold on which we all depend,
and you worked at your slippery trade till it left you dizzy
in the twilight of our economy, suitcases bulging with cash.

### Letter from an Old Physics Professor

I have always believed in precise mathematical laws
yielding clarity,
and that good water chemistry will save this environment.

I still believe that life and the mind
emerged from inanimate matter.

All my life I've made a serious study
of physics, and the subtle spin of small particles
within the heavy metals that seed our cancers.

But lately I've grown too absorbed in the mystery
of the red shift, measuring the emissions of distant supernovae
and looking back through time
to find the edge of the known universe,
the primordial first light.

I wonder at times if my science has forsaken me,
the reigning theory of gravity now dead, Einstein's vision
of relativity requiring some adjustments.

Have you ever wondered about the red-shifted light
that holds the key to winding the celestial clock?

Beyond the cosmic horizon the universe continues to expand,
and a peek behind the smooth curtain of radiation
reveals dark energy pervading all space and time,
a relic of Big Bang's fireball pushing the far-flung galaxies
further and further apart.

The Grand Designer's void is the same in all directions,
a puzzle inherent in the very fabric of the cosmos.

A radical colleague wrote the quest for these answers
through physics may be the gateway to a new religion,
one where all the ancient questions
are deemed unanswerable, and without form,
as shapeless as the wind in the reeds.

# Lethe

*From Quadrant, 2008*

My father drinks from the spring of forgetfulness.

Through the stillness of an afternoon, awash
with reminiscence, he pauses,
relatives long gone rising to whisper answers in his ear.

In his dreams they call to him
for an accounting, to enlighten the living.

The penumbra of his memory lumbers off
into far trees pulsing in the heat, while birds
levitate on afternoon thermals, spiraling upward.

Out there, he says,
beyond the smoky haze setting on the fields,
a barn is burning, fire consuming the cobwebs,
an ancient roof on the verge of collapse.

The ropy egg whites of his eyes
puzzle over past yearnings unfulfilled.

He says that he is uninterested
in comfort without the truth.

Those of us who linger on may be rewarded,
like scholars in a library, or explorers navigating
the far tributaries of a flow
who may, at times, find the lost or the forgotten.

Daily he walks a dark corridor for exercise,
pondering old photos framed on the wall.

At the end of that passage is a door
where he will find the solutions to all riddles.

My father is uninterested in comfort without the truth.

## Meditations after the Supernova

*From Quadrant, 2008*

The sun goes supernova and all that remains is beauty.

The blue and watery eye of our globe
blinks and disappears without an elegy or valediction.

Nothing escapes,
the masses evaporating
as one expression of heat and light.

All our oiled motion ends in a drifting thing of clouds.

Corruption whirls in a luminous well as the galaxy spins.

Infant stars
clump out of the infinite,
yet invisible magnetic flood.

Gravity bends time
and an ocean of gas arises to glow like a great lamp,
grand and serene, bright as any moon.

## Early Yellowing

Leaves of the cottonwoods yellow early.

The great white swans of Yellowstone
rise skyward in the twilight.

Eventually winter wins the final battle,
and weakened by the cold
you will look back at your follies and temptations,
puzzled by a vision of the future
where ozone levels speed us into oblivion.

Smoke rises out on the plains from an unknown source.

Our drunken neighbor's spooked mare races away
into the darkness of the trees.

In the icy blue of your eyes
I see the fading light of all our lost summers.

On a distant ridgeline, at this late hour,
a delicate mule deer turns our way to sniff the air.

## Return to Lindberg Pond

*2005*

The mushrooms are everywhere, urged upward by the rains,
tasty morels mixed in among the many, veiled death angels.

Not far from where you stand, veterans of Company C,
24th Iowa Volunteers, Grand Army of the Republic,
lie buried in an old, well groomed cemetery
shaded by a grove of cedars and a single, ancient basswood.

After the Civil War returning veterans found shelter here,
still burying those slow to die, and taking roll call
one last time at Lindberg Pond:

Thirty years ago this week South Vietnam fell,
a thing both quick and incomplete, where the events spoke
for themselves, a time that left you hovering like a dragon-fly,
listening forever to the dense whispers of those gun ships
skimming in low from the South China Sea.

The tiger salamanders make their way through the undergrowth,
pushing aside the may apples and jack-in-the-pulpits,
splashing through toxic run-off from a meth lab down the road.

This first cool week in May the migrating waterfowl
are slow to nest, as if they are unready for their annual cycle
among the reeds, and the silence of the frogs is a bit odd.

The brooding flickers call from the deep woods,
their zigzag flight looping in among the trees.

High in a tall hickory a red-tailed hawk dangles a bull snake,
her testy nestlings stretching out thin necks.

## Hidden Witness

Where the shy and iridescent mayflies hide,
tangling together among the ditch lilies,
two young lovers are taking off their clothes.

Time is a drum that beats within the deep woods.

And with the full blaze of high summer as a witness,
they connect in the shadows,
a light breeze lifting the heavy branches of the oaks.

Soon he is ready to slip away, easily startled into flight.

Out on the interstate he hears the tires of the big rigs
whining, heading west to unknown destinations,
the cough of a Detroit diesel backing down.

She shines as if linked to a divine source,
drowsy in the shade, lounging on a blanket in the nude,
as if they had all afternoon.

An unseen woodpecker raps a wake-up call on a distant trunk.

The delicate and glossy mayflies swirl upward in the gloom.

## Winter Moon

*For the last keeper of the ancient songs*

In Morrison, Colorado, a one-eyed half-blood lives alone,
still setting her snares for rabbits.

She follows the tracks of a subtle bobcat
to where the big cottonwoods shed golden leaves,
shaking a rattle made from turtle bones.

Her single eye has seen our future in the campfires,
when and where the clouds of ashes will smother the sun.

People pass on, she says, but the story doesn't end.

Even though her sons are dead
she sings her sublime songs for the ancient spirits
wandering among the trees.

Winter Moon, watch over us with your mystic, solemn eye,
and spare us from your dark prophesy.

Sing for us all with your exalted, celestial melodies.

## Hard Season

Back from both Afghanistan and Iraq,
you are out of money as the cold comes in, your rowdy friends
howling through the malaise, over at the Morrison Cantina.

Down in Denver people are out of work, old folks prowling
roadside ditches for soda cans, housewives clipping coupons,
and all the hot and tantric bitches from Littleton
hunting for lean, young men like you.

You are probably the last of high country cowboys,
a disabled veteran, and a true exile whose knee gave out
after a hard season riding rodeo.

In this economy you've learned to tangle with the cougars
coming out of Cherry Creek, those lawyers' wives
who transcend their separateness in the lull of an afternoon,
wrapping their legs around your waist for warmth.

## The Maize Goddess

*For Norman Dubie*

Once she was a vital force, imperious and unyielding,
who knew the place where the corn seed was hidden,
and where she would rendezvous with all the old men
wearing only an enchanted cloak to cover her nakedness.

She brought the rains to ease our yearnings every spring,
and in the winter her glowing hair streamed across the sky
beneath the Northern Lights, a promise of her return.

The Maize Goddess was the one true spirit rising
from those hallowed, dream-like realms
that only the shaman knew,
the ones anchored in the depths of time's deep seas.

Was it you who found her likeness strolling down a beach
along the Gulf of Mexico, possessing that radiant glow
of divinity which is the underlying reality of all things?

## The Crooked Truth

We catalog the insects in our garden,
checking a guide as evening comes on,
still wary of the devious spiders that lie in wait:

You marvel over the secret etiquette of the sugar glider,
the frantic ecstasy of a moth hovering above a wine glass,
the theory that all stars coalesce out of interstellar dust.

What if the arrow of time is a circle,
and the cobwebs in our garden the handiwork
of a cosmic sculptor playing upon a galactic scale?

The child in me still believes in magic,
that we all may be governed by an invisible energy,
an unknown hand that holds the cosmos in its grip.

How high-minded of me to spout off after a bottle of wine,
knowing outside our science nothing is ever clear-cut,
that what is most often true is in the glitches.

Let us trust those illusive inklings we have learned
on our own, those yearnings that once arose with a glance,
to be confirmed by the sweet blips and mishaps in our lives.

A honey-eater lingers over the red waratah
in the warp of the season's change,
feeding right up through twilight on these last, long days.

Those wild orange dogs in the distant thorn trees are restless,
ill at ease and always on guard in the horned and vicious dark,
living moment to moment with the crooked truth.

# In Gamoowea

*From Poetry Australia, 1976*

The honey-eater gathers with the shrike;
and I drink beer with my pregnant wife.

Stockmen speak of snow and ice,
hoarfrost in Tasmania,
of harvest nights layered with a freeze,
sound sleeping.

September is a native cat moving westward,
is the curl of a lizard
caked-hard in a dry creek-bed.

I say north of the MacDonell Range
these rolling hills are my woman's lap.

The stalks of stunted grass
are her underbelly's golden hair
sifted through the sand of the Barkly Tableland:

There are men opening graves in Queensland
and the Northern Territory, digging
for polished axe-heads of the long dead,
and there are chipped flints left unfinished
in Gamoowea, growing like a child's new cut teeth.

## Late Frost in Early Spring

*For D. H. Lawrence,*
*from Poetry Australia, 1976*

A frost is coming in
to shake the possum from a drowse.

Numb from the cold
adders tangle together under the ferns,
thick as human thigh bones.

The brooding adder revolves like a slow cylinder
to shed his skin,
and it awakes from the cold as a dumb loop
turned once
around the shaft of a sapling gum.

With a half-undone braid a thin girl is tickling
the slack edge of the snake's lip.

Over all the throats that snap and click
I can hear the bell-bird's whistle.

## Through Wingham Brush

*From Poetry Australia, 1976*

1

Picked up by a sea breeze
thin clouds spread inland over high, dark ridgelines.

A flying fox unwraps his wings in uppermost branches,
fanning the long leaves of a wild quince.

On the hard back above Wingham Brush
the moon is a child in dry grass, playing with matches.

2

We are sleepless as the wind picks up speed.

A dog
drops a crushed starling at our feet.

This is fire season.

In my wife's blond hair there are yellow leaves,
and insects slip inside her shirt.

3

Birds of the deep woods begin to sleep.

Cane toads grumble, waiting for a drizzle.

Across a river Queensland mingles with the smoke

of cooking fires,
and we await a storm.

Without a sound eucalypts shed their bark in strips.

February's flies are limbering young legs.

# Finding Africa on the Way to Broken Hill

*For Les Murray,*
*from Poetry Australia, 1976*

Call the black stump a lion's head.

For in the midday heat of the wide plains
small boys hear it roar.

Abandoned cars left on high ground
suggest rhinoceros at twilight;

And if you see tentative giraffes among the emus
crossing Nyngan's yellow flats,
you may have found Africa on the way to Broken Hill,
dust and dry water holes equal to the Velds:

I never saw the hot Zulu who broke my windscreen
with a stone, just outside Wilcannia.

Whirlwinds rose from a red salient.

Tire treads thick as elephant hide
were left in the footprint of a great truck.

## Slowly Waking

*From Poetry Australia, 1976*

Far out, in the Tasman Sea,
a thousand dolphins head south, under a full moon.

Across the street the post office is full of insects.

And grouped in close formations
lizards take command of the window screens,
are ready to advance:

This is Australia of the mile long beaches,
and tonight, as the parties end,
as the crowds turn out,
the mosquitoes are at the walls of the city,
the hibiscus explodes,
my wife turns in the empire of her sleep,
her stomach lunar,
slowly waking to a child's dolphin kick.

In the early morning schools of mullet move offshore.

The glint of small fish massing to spawn
flashes like rifle fire in the moonlit water.

## Looking for the Perfect Pilsner

For those who worship at the altar of the hops
our spirits are nourished
by the catkins of a twisted vine;

And often we find ourselves
breaking into song, the power of our voices
like the revelatory booming of the prophets,
enhanced by a fine, India Pale Ale.

What you hear is the din of our unwinding,
echoing down through the valleys, all of us
shaking off the effects of high country lassitude.

Who among us has not sought out the perfect Pilsner,
and heard the siren of Germanic legend, Loralei,
luring us back to the Rhine Bock, tempting us
through the sweet bloom of the Colorado summer?

We are the self-taught connoisseurs of the multitudes
and of the alehouses, remembering that the politics
of possibility first arose in a beer garden.

May we be the last left standing in our mountain halls,
aspirants still looking for that perfect Pilsner,
crafted to be clear and simple, limpid, marked
by a transparency, absolutely serene and untroubled.

## Part II: High Country

## The Spotted Colt

*From Turning Up The Leaves, 2000*

It was the heat that drove his lightning kicks.

When he leapt the gate his shoes struck sparks.

His dust
hung over the long track
like a spirit.

The runaway spun our afternoon about
to wake a light wind
who showed her slim belly by turning up the leaves.

High summer,
mother of June's blue hummingbird,
ready me for want of flight.

## Perhaps in Another Life We Were a Pair of Wolves

*From Buffalo Bones, 1998*

Once in that other life it rained.

And under a canopy of tall, coniferous trees,
by a lake where a wall of ferns
rose to shoulder-height, the moss, thick and green,
became a carpet to our rendezvous.

I remember the silence being broken by calls of birds,
and you turning to me with your bright eyes,
nuzzling close as the unseen birds responded
one to another, in a serenade for wolves.

We possess nothing but the here and now.

Recollections scatter through the mind
like flights of birds.

So when the howls carry across the canyons,
and there is only the darkness to embrace,
recall how you made me tremble,
and how what rushed through me
spilled into the flow of our heat and our becoming.

When that dark and eternal beast calls in the night,
think back to how we curled together.

When I am dead
think of how we once lived as wolves.

## A Walk in the Wetlands

*From Turning Up The Leaves, 2000*

Thousands of water creatures hum through the pools.

Transient jays shriek at your shadow.

We pass quietly
under the sacred antiquity of the cottonwoods;
for this is where we go to hide,
a journey over logs and millenniums of moss
to find what lies at the bottom of this wetland.

Here nature appears haphazard,
incidental as the water snake that blocks our path.

Wading through growth and decay
we feel blind to how things connect;
and we will always be interlopers to the frogs.

They scatter into the wet foliage, and, like us,
conceal themselves in sublime associations
with the leaves.

Bubbles of gas rise through splotches of algae,
nature's dark counterpoint
to the turbulent plumage of the oriole
and the swift iron-slick of the otter.

We move slowly into the coming night.

Small fish dart into hiding places
within the stagnant water.

The placid blossoms of the water lilies
are luminous at dusk,
like lamps on the water.

## On the Dakota Hogback

We come for the solitude,
knowing our own limitations, to watch the magpies,
and perhaps to observe, late in the day,
a golden eagle on a glide path home.

On the Dakota Hogback dirt bikes create disorder.

But here we feel the potent rhythm of emergence,
energy moving up to where energy needs to flow.

We blend into the jumble of rocks and juniper.

All about us magpies jump in a continuous dance.

A snake uncoils from the cold
in the keen subtleness
of the snake's craft.

Energies merge, and other wild things
shed winter like an old skin.

## Wolverine

Solitary and destructive,
victim of the bad rap,
few shed tears for the wolverine.

But you are fascinated by the skunk-bear,
fiercest
of the Grand Designer's children,
and stalk the edge of the tree line
to find where it fits.

Perhaps it's a matter of respect.

In this cold isolation
things fit with difficulty.

The truth
is that you get high on the action,
and what you are seeking
may be yourself.

You have been chasing tracks for years
only to lose the hot trail
again and again
to darkness or a weather change.

Once you came close,
catching a glimpse among the trees
on an opposite slope.

A dark shape was bounding away
against the whiteness of the snow.

## Eclipse

At the eclipse of the moon we walked
to where the pond lay still and deep.

And when a fox stirred in the leaves I froze,
long ago weathered by a war
and having surrendered to doubt.

We were lucky that the clouds had cleared
and for the fragrance of what bloomed unseen.

The drama of the moon's eclipse
might have escaped,
elusive as the fleeting eye-shine of that fox.

A night heron stood waiting,
unattended in the shadows,
his low and mundane call a melody to another,
while frogs croaked
and the rhythm of the night things
sounded in the chambers of the moon.

I have been too busy with day-to-day events,
with naked promises that pass us by;
and I have taken much for granted,
the cold torturer of facts,
having no time to ponder the moon's dark side
or that lunar shadow in the heavens
that whirled our heads.

## Prayer for the Bears

After a dry summer bear were coming down.

October had them confused, still hungry,
their hopes
tied
to imaginary garbage.

The dry summer had seen them proliferate
in spite of us,
impartial to our disorder and complaints,
a sow and two cubs
descending
as far as Lakewood.

It is said that bear never compromise.

But when a big male
tried to maul our dogs
someone sprayed him with a hose
and he ran,
bewildered,
to find refuge in the peace
of the dark spruce.

May he survive to enjoy
the full moon's moment,
and go back to scavenging road-kills.

May all the bear sleep, undisturbed,
in a dream time governed by their ancestors,
in caves deep within the Great Divide.

## Hunting for Antelope East of Yoder, Colorado

For an afternoon you share these dry plains
with occasional great stones that have no destination,
hunting for antelope
along a straight track crossed by wild dogs.

To your left
you are surprised by a snowy egret
descending from cool altitudes.

Along this flyway there are many possibilities,
and one overcomes the forgotten condition of the land,
the abandoned farms,
the accidents over which you have no control,
to find a form of comfort
when twilight rests on a far tableland.

We have all been struck by the sudden and unforeseen,
something wild as the intensity
that glows in the eye of another.

Overhead the egret rests in a lone cottonwood,
her black beak like a spike of dark crystal.

The great stones erode into odd and random shapes.

Here the distance and dust-haze favors the antelope,
and things cohere more by luck than design.

## At a Waterhole Along the Western Slope

You find that there is more here
than the hazed flatness of the land.

Deep below there are aquifers
that feed the waterhole,
and during the late afternoon
the yellow grass shimmers
to the meditations of the locusts.

At night,
when it is time to drink,
the languorous eyes of the mule deer
beg for mercy,
slipping by with their desires.

You play cards with the visiting multitudes,
under a camp's kerosene lamp.

Glazed stockmen,
weightless and without doubts,
their muscles hard as feldspar and galena,
spit at the immensity of the sky.

## Cutting Wood

In this high mountain valley,
for three days I searched the dry timber,
while our trucks
snapped through aspens
thick as tow cables.

Distant thunderheads
rose in the mountains to the west,
moving through the passes
with the porcupine.

The sweat and grit cut.

The features of each face were dust.

I believe only the airline pilots
truly understand this time,
and the different parts of the design.

Between the numbered hills and the high plains
they pass over me with their measured flights.

And while I cut wood
the rivers spread out on their electronic maps,
seemingly endless and immeasurable
slivers and spines.

In that open brightness everything is slick.

Eternity is a glistening impression.

## Voyager Two

Passing clouds unveiled the moon, and you stared,
lost in thought,
convinced that thinking late
could bring you to the truth
of whatever remained veiled.

As one finds limits to natural laws
you hoped to find a truth sublime as lynx eyes
shining in the dark.

There is no science to a rapt gaze;
nor is there a formula for dreams
across the distance of the night.

Where Voyager Two, gratified by chance,
visits Nepture and the unknown,
there are speculations that liberate small souls
and carry away generations
to an inspiration in the stars.

Inspire us, Voyager Two
beyond both our melancholy
and our smallness,
for your journey on the endless path is certain,
one lost in the heavens,
one never completed.

## The Calculus of Emotions

*From Turning Up The Leaves, 2000*

The calculus of emotions begins with the moon.

The nature of time
in intervals and intimacies of touch
is linked to motion.

I believe that the lunar curve holds the secret,
that the mystery is as it must be,
in the configurations of plants as they grow,
in the textures and colors of skins brought together,
in the spike of a shooting star.

The evolution of how we will be
is an outcome that always happens
in the darkness of the night,
and our feelings hold the promise of the future,
whenever we reflect.

I wonder if the matter of love
can be grounded earthward
in the rhythms that pulse through us
when we are ready to speed,
in tune with illuminations and phases in the sky?

Here the formulas and solutions are uncertain.

And I believe that we are designed to move
across great distances,
that there is a process
where we reveal ourselves in dreams.

That truth is still there, after all these years,
holding firm as a planet in an orbit,
perennial and absolute.

## High Country Solitudes

Occasional clouds
still close like scissors on the foothills.

December has been a damp month.

On cool nights the muzzles of buffalo
wire the air with vapor.

On clear nights
the stars guide your mind westward,
toward the high country solitudes.

Deep in the interior,
in the far distances,
your muscles still flex
on a blue mountain's backbone.

We all must live with the memory
of a journey never completed
or a path not taken.

As the sun sinks lower on the horizon
low pressure systems bring snow instead of rain.

The wet buffalo resting along the Genesee Exit
turn into dark haystacks.

## Listening Through the Silences: Nine Meditations

*For Itzhak Bentov*

1 – Breaking the Silence

Led by Octavio, that fallen-away Jesuit,
a pack of phony veterans ride their Harley-Davidsons
down Highway 285,
the thunder of their bikes echoing through the canyon;

And below, as far as you can see, the high plains
pitch and roll away, heavy swells surging eastward
to that ocean of the heartland.

So in the quiet of the early morning, after the bikers
are gone, you begin your climb
to where the ocean of the plains meets the mountains.

You walk a trail used for centuries by the cliff-dwellers,
hiking to where the high ridges
and deep caves hide their secrets.

You believe in a subtle vibration that permeates all things;

And you may have even heard the hum of the universe
where the spiritual teachers of the cliff-dwellers
gathered for their awakenings.

Why is it you have kept to yourself for so many years?

Where now is that diverse caste of fine young officers
with whom you once served?

2 – The Sculptor

Always you go when the feeling comes, hiking the backcountry.

Turn too far inward, and you fall out of touch, lose capacity,
find yourself alone and listening to the silences.

You descend once again to where the darkness pushes in,
your receiver on adjusted amplification,
tuning into the mellifluous flow of history,
picking up the debris of the long dead:

At the edge of a cliff dwelling
you pause at a well filled with refuse of the ages,
a rubbish hole left by the ancients
where your friend Karl has been working
on the same sculpture for thirty years.

Karl tells you there is no free ride,
and that the current malaise will pass,
the wobbly economy restored by our endless war.

He chisels at the crumbling sandstone
into the twilight, to begin again in the morning
until he gets it right.

As the darkness comes on he claims all his representations
are imperfect, indefinite and unformed conceptions,
the ideal being that hot newscaster, Roxanne,
whom he compares to Alexander's queen,
or perhaps a modern siren modeled after that bitchy Chelsea,
the blonde spectacle from New Jersey.

Karl's cancer is terminal,
and once this old friend has passed
your only hiking companion will be the wind.

### 3 – The Janus-Faced God

Karl and I served that Janus-faced God of Steel,
the one who seduced us all with those false promises.

Don't tell me that there is hope for him,
lost in his shack back in these foothills.

He is one of the many, who have lived their lives alone,
always locked and loaded, and looking back,
crawling down into the narrow tunnels of their minds.

From Golden, Colorado's Tin Cup Trailer Court
and the West Colfax motels, to Denver's high rise towers,
a miscellany of veterans whirl far out on the edge of things,
in the Kuiper Belt of their old memories.

When Karl and I reach the caves
the echoes of our footsteps stir a thousand wings:

And backed into a great chamber we learn once more
the lesson of their resting places, how quickly bats
rise skyward toward the light.

A single wing brushes your intruder's face.

Streaks of dung stripe the cave walls, clusters
of bats writhing in a formless mass, a thousand-headed snake
disintegrating, streaming away into the depths, one by one.

The slick floor of this cave,
once the bed of an ancient sea,
glistens against the violence of our bright lights,
and the fierce reflections in the multitudes
of their eyes lasts only for a moment.

4 – Purple Sand

There is a pattern and design
to the great Morrison Formation,
sedimentary rocks containing dinosaur tracks;

And in the purple sand from broad flood plains
laid down by long dead rivers there are crocodile teeth
that appear like diamonds.

The tilt and buckle of the rocks is a puzzle to be solved.

Tell your daughters that faith will solve the divine mystery.

Tell them that here meaning becomes clear over time,
in the events that make up our lives,
and that relativity is the cosmological constant,
the force that props up the universe.


5 - The Ocean of the Night

Lately you worry about consequences,
for now, with your bad heart, time in not irrelevant.

In your sleep you dream across the ocean of the night,
and in your dreams, boulders of red sandstone,
ages-old sandstone, cast shadows across a valley.

Always you awake to find things undone, the natural cycle
upset, and a moth, fluttering before your face,
causes you to spring in terror from the bed.

Keep your perspective, you say:

When our sun shrinks back to become a white dwarf
the lingering death could last a trillion years.

6 – Observing the Rattlesnakes

In the lull of an afternoon
you sort through volcanic ash.

Once there were lagoons in this dry basin,
marine crocodiles the size of semi-trailer trucks
pondering the curve of the universe.

Now the rattlesnakes doze
on the afternoon's broad, flat rocks;

And in the geological record
you find motion captured in stone,
the ripple marks of ancient sea beds,
the action of the waves
fossilized into sensuous curves,
the fluid snakes as they back away,
wrapping into coils, ready to strike.


7 – Observing a Plain of Shimmering Grass

This is the foothill's transition zone
where remnants of the tall grass prairie
reach first soils of the Jurassic.

Further west fossils of long dead invertebrates
turn up on dusty roads;
and you know that the brontosaurus once danced
where zonked-out skateboarders now spin.

You sit in meditation, watching the hawks
circle at twilight,
the silky herds of antelope
wandering across a plain of shimmering grass
as old as the Cretaceous.

Have no doubt that the sun will eventually collapse

upon itself, afterwards swelling to engulf
the inner planets until our oceans boil.


## 8 – The Invisible Zones

Before the fire, at a campsite once used
by the last chief of the Utes,
you listen through the silences.

This is when the owl travels through invisible zones
to the other end of time;

And when the snake, so complete and true to itself,
sleeps quietly with the ocean of its own chance dreams,
having taken in the heat of the day,
only to be strengthened and reconciled
by those rhythms of the land that never change.

## 9 – The Ninth Meditation

The dense gases and star clusters
of the Milky Way glow overhead;
and Orion draws his long bow across the sky.

Connected to some other place in the larger scheme
you try to forget the anger within, letting everything flow,
slipping the boundaries through meditation.

Maybe it is true that divinity lies dormant within us,
a mystery waiting to rise again from the ages,
from the marble pagodas of Vietnam to these eroded sandstone
shapes once worshiped by the Utes:

My friend, Klaus, the nominalist,
believes the universal essences of reality are a fiction,
and that the mind can frame no single concept
to any valid term or corresponding image.

I disagree, having seen Evil hanging in the trees,

with tangled guts out and swinging in the breeze,
a sickening validity found in those private parts
still left bloody and fly-ridden on the ground.

In the black infinitudes of the night
the bones of that giant hunter slain by Artemis
rest in a glinting ossuary hidden among the stars;

And when our sun finally explodes
the earth in its death throes
will become a dead husk, all our remains
mere embers in the great galactic arc.

## In an Arid and Sun-Burnt Place

This bright and cloudless morning
you have a great view of the sandstone formations
called the Red Rocks, monoliths older than the Jurassic.

But looking out your window you could just as well
be trekking across a forgotten, dusty plain, back
searching those shallow and nameless rivers of your memory.

In an arid and sun-burnt place, half a world away,
the news reported a tragedy that went down while you slept:

A young girl was stoned to death for not marrying an old man.

When do such actions become crimes against humanity?

Over time the haunting images of her death will rise
to trouble your dreams, and you wish there were divine spirits
who had the power to intervene in such affairs.

At times you yearn to be swept up in the passion
of a Rapture, to liberate all those souls, and to truly believe
once again in some greater purpose than yourself.

The current media feeds a craze for vampires and social misfits,
and even the profane wish to cross that River of Promises
where all might take their ease and wash themselves clean.

Half a world away, in an arid and sun-burnt place,
the tragedies continue to unfold while you awake.

## From a Letter at Winter Solstice

*From Buffalo Bones, 1998*

Two coyotes track a bloodline in the snow.

Knee-deep in a drift's undulations
a wounded elk
stumbles on the endless path.

We traverse a high ridgeline,
keeping our distance at winter's solstice,
knowing that there is no hope
without trust.

Today death is the only promise kept
in this landscape, and the elk circles,
captured in the net of time,
restitution for the ravens that have found him.

Let us find the sparks in the darkness.

Let us learn to dance without a guide,
to raise our eyes to the stars.

The howl of the coyote is a requiem.

## Chinook

This morning, at daybreak,
the Chinook is at war with the trees,
thrashing through the willow's branches
to eat the last of January's ice.

I am sitting motionless at the table,
waiting for coffee,
remembering how our faces
touched in the darkness,
and how our rhythm
powered
a spark that flowed through us.

In the span of a lifetime
there are forces that combine
to leave their mark,
and this morning,
as time speaks
through the wind and the bent grasses
emotion is reason enough for being.

Outside the returning birds
flying before the wind
own the nameless stars,
taking their direction
from the emerging light on the horizon's edge.

Do you hear time speaking to them
through the wind and the bent grasses,
repeating that love
is never aimless when it lifts the spirit?

## Winter Light

*For Cheryl*

In that moment of extremes outside of Georgetown,
when the Ford ahead of us spun under the heavens,
in the cold winter light
we saw a life-time of trade-offs
weighed in an instant.

Where the miners took a chance to find a lode of silver
we found a roadside ditch.

And motionless in a snowdrift,
I suddenly awoke to fragile connections.

At a spot where some became wealthy
and others died penniless,
where gamblers and prostitutes
once fed on the promise of a boomtown's future,
our own history confronted a slick highway.

Yes, it is a random universe,
but it is clear that in the natural order
and in the passing of time,
love occurs between the sky's emptiness and despair.

So let us have no regrets
in a world where control is an illusion.

For we are living here and now,
and we have found a warmth rare
in a world of our own distinctions, in the winter light.

## Elegy for the Gulf of Mexico

*After the prophecy in Revelation 8:8\**

The Mesoamerican Doomsday is not a joke.

The nine lords of the Mayan night await us
strung out on meth, beckoning across the ages
from the crumbling pyramids of Tikal.

These days are now nameless for we have closed
their sacred Almanac of the Dead:

I am convinced that the cosmic shift
is not a fabrication, nor a chance happening.

We are at the long-anticipated zenith
by my calendar, the one I carry in my sacred bundle,
and whose text only I can read.

A one-eye cat creeps through my apocalyptic dreams.

His eye reflects the glaciers melting down,
fires sweeping through the Australian Outback,
blood and fire in the Gulf of Mexico.

The portals between our mortal realm and the Underworld
are opening slowly now, oil oozing out of the depths, up
from that opaque quiet of the deep where the Kraken sleeps.

*\* And the second angel sounded, and as it were a great
mountain burning with fire was cast into the sea: and the third
part of the sea became blood; Revelation 8:8*

## Return to Wingham Brush

*From Quadrant, 2010*

You stroll under the dense canopy,
returning to where the flying foxes take their ease,
your winsome guide light-on-her-feet,
a sun-burnt ember unprepared for her own perfection.

Once again you are traveling through old territory,
where the dung-striped roots fulminate and decay,
and thirty years ago this week
you drained a case of Flag Ale.

The Strangler Figs rise like pillars in a great temple,
while the sheltered multitudes, suspended high above,
fan themselves through the flies and heat, peering down
with their unblinking gaze, fixed and fluorescent in the gloom.

Your guide leads you up a path in the euphoria of the twilight,
telling you of her rigorous voice training,
of how she hopes to tour Europe with its promise of liberation,
much to her father's discontent.

One by one the flying foxes take flight above their sanctuary,
holding roll call and whispering their secrets,
forming into an ascending spiral while your guide shares
the tale of how they hung Jimmy Governor.

The undulating shadow gathers momentum in the dusk,
a wavy line breaking off and stretching away as far
as you can see, a crooked truth swinging in the dark,
melting into time's hazy, immeasurable distances.

Overwhelmed by what you have witnessed, you sit in silence,
wondering if she knows about Jimmy's wife, of how
our choices define us, with mothers losing track of daughters
and best friends parting company, their marriages gone awry.

Do you dare tell her that we are the thuggish agents of desire,
the opaque instruments of all we have left undone,
our story but an extension of so many imperfections,
guided by the cruel infinity loop of our persistent dreams?

## Crop Circles

*After N.S.W. 2008*

Hardly a mention of crop circles these days in the news,
the interpretations of what is happening usually contradictory.

All we really have are the traces at the scene, evidence
of a thing drawn in an expansive arc, a truth inaccessible
through the internet, and you wonder what shameful crime
has been committed on your consciousness.

We are all victims of irrationality in some form,
yanked around by jealous gods in the media.

The spontaneous forces that prompt our actions in the markets
are akin to the divine mystery.

How deep do you dig in your pockets to find a coin
for that disabled veteran panhandling on the street,
the one without any legs, scooting himself along
on a curiosity made from old plywood and tiny wheels?

The tribes gather to tell their stories
up in the Northern Territory;

And as the global economy speeds toward collapse,
the economists spin their tale of what is going down.

## Elegy for a Lost Comrade

*After N.S.W. 2008*

Your sister wrote me that when they brought you back
the burial was held in a tiny graveyard
away from the beaten track,
at a place called Jamberoo.

I brushed off those fossils I still had
of our shared experiences, my mind wrapped around
those particulars from another time and place,
hoping for perspectives leading to broader truths.

Do you suppose that the past is truly unsalvageable,
an entity like the body of a soldier beheaded
by a masked enemy, the head later discovered
in a ditch, its eyes squeezed shut forever?

The last I heard you were drilling down through history
into the bedrock, sinking a well in an off-beat spot
where the travelers never stop,
still recovering from that ill-defined, forgotten war.

You ramble now in the company of ghosts,
gathered with all the lost to climb that clock tower
of the night, the one rising above the ruins
in the wilderness of the cities.

Logging in the names of my comrades, I still hear their voices,
the ones pure and undiminished that arise from what remains,
and I will listen while the clock ticks
for your greeting from the other side.

## Elegy for a Rare Forest Antelope

*From Operation Oklahoma Hills, May 1969\**

You enter a zone where the trees soar skyward,
blocking out the sun,
working your way along a massive ridge.

Vines thick as a man's thigh twist upward into the trees,
and in places you are up to your waist in swirling fog.

When you reach the crest of the ridge
the view is staggering, a vast landscape broken
by deep ravines, with rugged limestone karsts
jutting above a green expanse.

Who knows what is hiding from you in the dense canopy,
where the sanctuaries and forbidden base camps
number in the hundreds, and await your discovery?

The mountains looming in the west belong to Laos.

To the east a plume of smoke marks a contact.

The sun glints off the tail of a distant aircraft
making its bomb run across the valley floor far below,
where the Agent Orange has done its work, leaving
a barren swath, pock-marked with water-filled craters.

Your gaze locks on the plane's descent, and across
that leafless moonscape, outrunning the air strike,
a lone forest antelope gallops for the safety of the trees.

*\* Years later, the rare forest antelope sighted on Operation
Oklahoma Hills was identified as a Saola, a species yet to be
described by science. Today fewer than 300 of these solitary
creatures remain along the Laotian/Vietnamese Border, an
area that saw extensive use of Agent Orange defoliant.*

## Crossings

*Remembering Vietnam, 1968-70*

For forty years you have been crossing a river.

Your smooth companion
has been the dark,
and many a night, along the riverbank,
you have turned circles
in the tall grass to make a bed.

Tonight brings back a memory of the monsoon,
and you awake in a zone where ridgelines
rise like weapon-heaps,
study the landscape
till the violence snaps back.

Time grows into the tall grass,
and distance becomes an endless fence.

For you there will be no homecomings
to where the razor edge of the elephant grass
scratched your cheek,
and you have grown a beard no lover would recognize
should time ever bring you both face to face.

On your flank there will always be a murmur,
and moving out from the tangle of the thickets
you will always pick your steps.

What you carry in this crossing is that dark weight
that broke us all apart, a weight you feel even now
when the full moon's rise fixes your gaze.

We are all destined for some measure,
if not by being lost,
then by bearing the dark weight home.

## About the Author

Dan Guenther was a captain in the U.S. Marine Corps. His Lost Vietnam trilogy, *China Wind*, (Ivy, 1990) (Redburn, 2007), *Dodge City Blues* (Redburn, 2007), and *Townsend's Solitaire* (Redburn, 2008), is based on his combat experiences in Vietnam. His award-winning fourth novel, *Glossy Black Cockatoos* (Redburn, 2009), is a roman' a clef set in Australia and Southeast Asia following the Fall of Saigon in 1975. Dan has a BA in English from Coe College and a Masters of Fine Arts in English from the University of Iowa where he attended the Iowa Writers' Workshop. www.danguenther.com

## About Redburn Press

This is the newest Redburn Press title.  Redburn Press gets its name from the early Melville novel.  In it, the autobiographical narrator goes to sea for the first time, excitedly.  The ship is full of fascinating types, eccentric human nature in its motley richness.  Wellingborough Redburn then encounters more "life and life only".  I want Redburn Press to be that ship in a bottle, so to speak. I will publish – and republish --- eclectic, various, good books full of life.  Dan Guenther's *The Crooked Truth* is such a book.

*China Wind*, *Dodge City Blues*, and *Townsend's Solitaire*, the three books of the Dan Guenther's Vietnam Trilogy, as well as his award-winning fourth novel, *Glossy Black Cockatoos* (Redburn, 2009), are still available from Redburn Press online or through your local bookstore.

Mark Kohut
Publisher
October 2010